Through Ebony Eyes

By

Ivery L. Henderson

authorHOUSE

1663 LIBERTY DRIVE, SUITE 200
BLOOMINGTON, INDIANA 47403
(800) 839-8640
www.authorhouse.com

First published by AuthorHouse 09/15/04

ISBN: 1-4184-5391-9 (e)
ISBN: 1-4184-3797-2 (sc)

Printed in the United States of America
Bloomington, Indiana

This book is printed on acid-free paper.

In dedication to my mother,
Mary, who died at 85, and
her 6 children who survive.

TABLE OF CONTENTS

AMERICA 1

ALASKA 2

THE POSTMAN..3

THESE PARTIES 5

DON'T FORGET YOUR ROOTS 6

HI-TECH..7

HUNGER..8

THE WORLD NEEDS A SMILE..9

I AM...10

SISTERS THREE 11

LOVE IS 12

LIVE 13

ODE TO A POSTAL SCAB..14

OUR TABLE..15

GROW UP 16

JUSTICE — INJUSTICE 17

WHO'S RUNNING THE COUNTRY? 18

THE LAW 19

THE GREATEST TEACHER 20

THE WHOLE IS NO BETTER THAN ITS PARTS 21

THE BEST DAY 23

MONEY..24

WOMAN...25

MY DAUGHTER, HIS WIFE 26

DOUBLE MINDED 28

A CRY FROM THE GRAVE...30

GONE IN THE FLESH, ALIVE IN THE SPIRIT 32

STAIR, STEPS AND CHILDREN 33

HER BEAUTY PROVOKES MY LOVE 34

RUNNERS TAKE YOUR MARK 36

MY BEDROOM 37

HAPPY AND EMOTIONAL WOMAN.......................................38

MY BROTHER.......................................39

HURT 40

I DREAM OF GENIE.......................................41

LIFE GIVER.......................................44

IN YOUR FACE 45

ALL ON THE GOODFOOT 46

THE FIRST LOVE 47

REFLECTION 48

GOD CREATED.......................................49

HAVE A HEART 50

HAVE A GOOD DAY.......................................51

I AM AFRAID 52

FEAR 53

NATURAL BIRTH 54

CHILDREN 55

WIND.......................................56

THE BOXER 57

THE GREATEST BOXER EVER LIVED.......................................58

THE GREATEST ATHLETE 60

WHO'S TO BLAME? 61

IT'S IN THE EYES 63

WHO IS SHE?.......................................64

WHY DO I LOVE YOU?.......................................65

GENTLENESS 67

I CAN.......................................68

HE IS MY BROTHER.......................................69

TOGETHERNESS...70

HOME...71

LONELINESS 72

HE CARES 73

LOVE IS LIGHT 74

AGAIN...75

UNFORESEEN VIOLENCE..76

DAMAGE FROM WITHIN 77

THE CLEVEREST MAN..78

MY LOVE...79

CHILDREN GONE, DADDY STILL HOME 80

WHEN MY WIFE CRIES 81

COVER UP..82

TIME WILL TELL 83

EGOTISTICAL MAN 84

SPECIAL 85

CAUSE I KNOW YOU 86

UP JUMPED THE DEVIL 87

NEVER GIVE UP...88

YOUR DOG..89

MARRIAGE 90

THE CHURCH 91

THERE MUST BE A BALANCE 92

STANDS TO REASON 93

IN THE SHADOW 94

TINTED 95

WORDS 96

IT'S NOT OVER 97

THE BARNYARD PIMP..98

THE TELEPHONE...99

SHE IS A BRICKHOUSE 100

LET US THINK FOR OURSELVES 101

IN THE BAR 102

IN THE BAR 103

GRANDMOTHER 104

LADY OF THE HOUR 106

HE COME FROM AMONG US 107

PEOPLES CHOICE...108

THE FACE OF A CLOWN...109

WILLIE THE WEASEL 110

HE CAME GUNNING 111

FEELINGS...112

NOTHING COMES EASY 113

CHICKEN..114

MY TRIP HOME 116

WHAT IS THERE TO LOOK FORWARD TO IN LIFE
BESIDES GOD?..117

IN MY WORLD 119

THE MIND KNOWS 120

WHY NOT A SPANKING?...121

POWER TO THE PEOPLE...122

THE BRIDE AND GROOM 124

MY SISTER'S HOME..125

IN THE CLOUDS...126

BAYOU ST. JOHN 127

TRIPPING AND HOPPING MY FLIGHT HOME 128

IN THE END 133

AMERICA

America, A nation where others seek to come.
America, A nation where people are united as one.
America, A nation larger than the eye can see.
America, A nation where freedom is being free.
America, A nation where the free are full of pride.
America, A nation where soldiers fought and died.
America, A nation whose people are so diverse.
America, A nation that stands for Peace on Earth.
America, A nation filled with great tradition.
America, A nation carrying out a worldly mission.
America, A nation first in might and power.
America, A nation of the hour.
America, A nation where you won't be disappointed.
America, A nation that God has blessed and anointed.
America, One of many nations.
Americans, blessed by God but few among the nations of **people.**

ALASKA

She is big and beautiful. Men the world over, come to her because she is highly valued. She is a diamond in the rough. Her sisters are far away, yet they will never be able to physically touch her. Some love her and others envy her. She was born late but she has more to offer than any one of them. Whatever the reason they don't want her to go at it alone. She has managed to do better at taking care of herself but like a mother who won't let go of you even after you have matured, she has been given limitations. Her ancestors look to her for shelter and food. Newcomers come to her for a better life. Businesses seek her resources and wealth. If you don't seek to know her ways, she can be your bitter enemy. She can change like the four seasons all in one day. She is an extremist in the winter and a sunshine of love in the summer. Her beauty seems to never end. She changes from beauty to beauty during the seasons of the year, yet she gives an offering. Her waters are rich, rugged and raging, yet she can't be tamed. Her tides roll in the way a woman rolls her hair, outward. She is so fertile that what she produces or whoever eats what she produces grows larger than the norm. You must always give her respect or she will take your life.

She is the Great One

THE POSTMAN

The postman is a customer's friend.
He delivers mail with a smile and a grin.
Some letters are personal, others are business.
Behind each delivery is caring and friendliness.
The postman is responsible for serving a route.
His knowledge of people's behavior is what gives him clout.
Many of the customers, carriers treasure
Their loving kindness is beyond measure.
Some customers will lie to you and mourn.
Others display behavior that'll open your arms.
At times they make accusations expressed as fact.
Supervisors, without proof, put the monkey on your back.
These managers and supervisors state workers don't listen.
The fact is, carriers are placed in an awkward position.
Supervisors seek to control by scare tactics and fear.
They never give instructions that are perfectly clear.
Most get engrossed in computers to keep you on track.
They use this information to stab you in the back.
Managers have not learned from the past.
Human relations, at its best, complete the task.
New workers, they carry for an 89-day stint.
Supervisors fire them without a clue or hint.
As autocratic managers their thinking is insensitive.
Forgetting such thinking causes you to be defensive.
Their abuse of authority continually affects morale.
Most carriers have desires to ring management's bell.
When you give them input you are accused of scheming.
They follow up with action that is very demeaning.
Yes, one supervisor gives you a task.
Another follows with instructions that clash.
When you get back to the workroom floor.
Managers rush to get you out the door.
Like vultures, screaming, "Get off the clock"
The post office should review managers in position.
And fill these slots with mangers who listen.

3

Good communication both ways would produce a superb system.

THESE PARTIES

They call themselves Republicans and Democrats.
History shows they used Whites against Blacks.

The one in power makes promises he can't keep.
Their filibustering have dulled the people to sleep.

They are continually waging war with their jaws.
The people awake to find both parties have committed fraud.

The poor continues to be poor as the rich ask for more.
Yet politicians prove to be the people's biggest foes.

Parties state "Vote" we'll look out for every woman and man.
After all is said their action show they don't give a damn.

One will use religion to express being morally correct.
Forgetting, while his party was in office, it created the mess.

Either party is master at playing the political game.
They totally forget about the common woman and man.

Politicians are like crabs in a bucket struggling for the top.
The other sees the struggle and insures the other is stopped.

Both claim if elected the people we will serve.
Once elected the people are never heard.

Most politicians are lawyers or have wealth.
They bleed us with taxes as we struggle with out health.

Servants are supposed to work for their master.
Yet, American people are treated like illegitimate bastards.

They serve, they serve themselves.
This is their Moral Agenda.

DON'T FORGET YOUR ROOTS

Too young brother, you weren't around.
The 60's are when your rights were found.
60's Blacks were struggling for freedom,
Riding in the back seat of a bus and by police beaten.
Black leaders were meek, mild, and dogmatic,
Seeking at all measure to be democratic.
Although the emancipation proclamation was signed in 1863,
You couldn't say the Black man was free.
Black leaders were truly the best of men;
They fought hard for our rights and were at the forefront to defend.
When the system made promises, but wouldn't budge.
Martin Luther King, Ralph Abernathy, Elijah Muhammed, Andrew
Young,
Stokley Carmichel, Dick Gregory, Malcolm X, Benjamin Hooks,
Thurgood Marshall,
H. Rap Brown, and Jessie Jackson would all vocally give a
thoughtful nudge.
There were many more, too many to mention.
These were at the forefront tending the store.
They never forgot who they were, or where they came from.
They wanted society to offer their people more than a mop and a
broom.
Society would have you think these men started the mess.
If it weren't for them, you wouldn't be blessed.
They weren't looking out only for Blacks;
They were working to get the American society back on track.
Don't forget your heritage; remember where you came from.
Accomplish all that you can so that you won't have to push a mop
or broom.
Refuse to live life as a sleeper,
Have keen ears listening to the words of teachers and preachers.

HI-TECH

Hi-tech has sought to subvert God's plan.
Using the lab to create future woman and man.

God placed in man a desire for ethics.
Hi-tech seeks to control life's genetics.

God structured man to procreate through sex.
Hi-tech wants power to determine who is next.

Scientific research has forgotten the moral issue.
Hi-tech interest is focused on fetal tissue.

Instead of science solving the issues of life.
Hi-tech discoveries continue to bring mankind strife.

They no longer look to God our creator.
All they seek comes for the use of data.

HUNGER

The children, they cry out
Their spirits broken.
Their little bodies undernourished.
Their eyes bulging.
Their faces withdrawn.
And their stomachs swollen.
Feed me, feed me.
As their inner strength is sapped.
Withstanding the pains of hunger
Their souls wonder why, why.
With all the resources of the earth
Surrounding them
Leaders caught up in the world
Caring for money, power and instruments of destruction.
Forgetting helping the sick and poor would
Serve a godly function.
Life would be so much better if the simplest
Things were provided.
Food and the Word
True Life.

THE WORLD NEEDS A SMILE

A Smile is what the world needs.
Each exchange puts others at ease.
It gives off warmth yet it won't burn.
Brings happiness, for which the world yearns.
A smile removes sadness from a face.
And to your head adds a halo of grace.
A smile should never be feigned.
Receiver can interpret what a smile means.
When smiling be sure it's from the heart.
A forced smile will reveal your thought.

I AM

I am not who you think I am.
You won't let me be.
If I was who you think I am.
I would not be me.
If you let me be.
I would give my love free.
All the world would know.
I'd keep coming back for more.
I'd love you as before.
For I'd know what's in store.
Wake up the time is right.
We don't have to fight.
Our love is just and right.
As we trust each other with all our might.
Instead of being right all the time.
We would come together as one mind.

SISTERS THREE

My sisters consist of three.
They are Lydia, Emelda and Mary.
Mary is the oldest.
She's smart, tough and boldest.
Following Mary was Lydia Jean,
First maid to the high school queen.
Lydia was full of knowledge,
First sister to complete college.
Emelda was the baby.
No way was she lazy.
Her smile was quick and simple.
She displayed beautiful dimples.
Emelda was thinner and smallest.
She was also the tallest.
My sisters are now grown ladies.
All were excellent mothers to their babies.
They raised their children with love and tact,
To this day, my sister need not look back.

LOVE IS

Love can be expressed in a smile.
Love can be expressed in kindness.
Love can be expressed in giving.
Love returned gives a reason to keep living.

Love causes the loved one to feel good.
Love causes the loved one to share.
Love causes a dog to give his master devotion.
Love is an expression that is active in motion.

Love to each of us is not the same.
Love to each of us is witness on three planes.
Loves to each of us is experienced physically,
Mentally and spiritually at its best.
Love to each of us causes bonding of our spirit,
Body and soul, a truth that we are blessed.

LIVE

You can live a life of love
If you love the life you live.

In both, loving and living
A part of you is giving.

To really live
You must forgive.

Forgiving, you are showing you care
From the heart coming, makes you share.

Sharing, caring and forgiving
Produces wholesome loving and living.

ODE TO A POSTAL SCAB

Scabs are not for but against.
To the union, this doesn't make sense.
If they only knew of the contribution by the union.
Contribution that has kept management's tricks from abusing them.
The scab does not pay dues.
Yet, it is of his free will that he chooses.
Scabs continuously reap union members' benefits.
Though he brown nosed to be part of management click.
Management continued to erode away rights.
Scabs must realize by himself he cannot fight.
Most scabs end up supervisors you see.
Look around, few become 204 B's.
Think you got it made being a scab?
You are standing for nothing,
You've been had.

OUR TABLE

Our table is a place to give thanks, eat and share.
Our table is a place surrounded by chairs.

Our table is a place where food is placed.
Our table is a place we bow our head and say our grace.

Our table is a place the Lord makes his presence known.
Our table is a place where our house feels like a home.

You can sit at our table for many a reason.
The purpose our table serves is always in season.

GROW UP

He made you and me out of the earth.
He gave us life so we would acknowledge him.
He called us friends for our bodies are the temples of God.
If we don't obey to all the things we just heard,
Temptation will be great and Satan will await.
Yet some people use drugs as a way to escape.
So called friends say, "Cocaine makes you feel great."
Yet it is because of this you can lose your faith.
These lies are perpetrated by the enemies of truth.
When all is said and done you are of no use.
Too many times we get caught up in the things that give pleasure.
Forgetting that our maker and creator is who we should treasure.
Drugs bring hurt to your body and also disease.
Satan sees you in this state and he's pleased.
Drugs will tear you down; Jesus will lift you up.
Drugs may take you to flight; Jesus will give you life.
One of these days Jesus will call you to confess.
If you are in accordance with his word, you will be blessed.
If not, you don't get a second chance.

JUSTICE — INJUSTICE

Is justice in America really fair?
Lawyers do everything to get criminals spared.
They do everything to keep the white collar criminal in chains.
Hard core criminals are back preying off the land.
Lawyers plea-bargain on the convict's behalf.
Making the injustice committed a thing of the guilty plea,
But the justice – injustice let them go free.
This is not true justice, but a numbers game.
Lawyers getting fat off the people of the land.
Rich and the affluent can pay for their crime.
To the lawyers money is the sign.
No! Justice is not fair; ask any lawmaker.
Look what justice of the world did to Jim Baker.
Yes, he committed a crime and he sinned.
He was not destructive to the whole of society.
As Michael Miliken.
Miliken was in the in-crowd; he stole millions, or was it billions?
The people were astonished.
Compared to Jim Baker he was mildly admonished.
You call that justice? No!
Justice – Injustice

WHO'S RUNNING THE COUNTRY?

Does America belong to the people? I'd like to know.
My perception makes me think we are being snowed.
We the people of the U.S. should own our own money and our
banks.
The International Bankers have caused our society to sink.
Like a bunch of cattle in a herd,
We are controlled by the Federal Reserve.
Stop and think!
Federal Reserve is owned by the International Bank.
Be no fool, Federal Reserve is the International Bank tool.
The Federal Reserve can pay $23.00 per 1000 notes.
This includes the cost of printing, paper, ink, and labor, so
despicable I want to choke.
This is a small price. Do you think it is right?
Signed by the treasurer, secretary of the treasury, this is another
joke.
These individuals have no power on these notes.
Don't it stink!
Federal Reserve is neither owned nor operated by the U.S.
Government.
The Bureau of Engraving and Printing has no control over the
Federal Reserve.
The International Bank always has the last word.
So we the people have to beg, borrow, or steal;
Not knowing where we are going to get our next meal.
No wonder Americans feel jumpy.
Who is really running this country?
While we are working hard to do what is right,
All big businesses take a flight.
As soon as we try to get our finances in order,
Businesses pull out and run for the border.
Who's running the country?

THE LAW

True laws of a society should be based on what is right and what is
true.
Not if you got money.
Not if you are affluent.
Not if you are poor.
Not if you are Black or White.
But if what is true and right.
Laws are made for man.
But lawbreakers have more rights and privileges and don't give a
damn.
Decisions and justice are not fair in courts.
Too often the power of the people has been given to law
enforcement.
And abuse by police has become the norm.
At times use vice and corruption instead of righting the wrong.
If the law doesn't respect the rights of the people,
The people have no desire to respect the law.
Because of illegal tactics you become a pawn
In the justice system that holds you in its paw.
You become like what is.
It becomes you.
Through word and deed.
This is what society breeds.
Inhumane treatment, what police do to one color in the end,
Will be done to all colors of men.
A development of a police state all people will become victims.

THE GREATEST TEACHER

He was born in a manger.
People of his time considered him a stranger.
His life was programmed by God from a child to a man.
This was inclusive of God's plan.
The greatest teacher that ever lived.
His whole life was based on the word give.
He came into the world as the redeemer of men.
To buy them back from the world's sin.
He taught us not to commit acts of stealing.
Due to his compassion, he would supply spiritual healing.
This child was God's gift to the world.
As the child lived, you could see it unfold.
He was patient, loving, and obedient to others.
In all things he gained favor with the father.
He was baptized.
Yet, by men, he was despised.
He healed the sick; touched the eyes of the blind,
And cast out demons at ease.
And in doing so, the Father said, "This is my beloved son in whom
I am well pleased."
To some, he was considered a prophet and a preacher,
To the world our Christ and Lord is the greatest teacher.

THE WHOLE IS NO BETTER THAN ITS PARTS

Whether it is a country or the human body,
The whole is no better than its part.
When one is sick with a life threatening disease,
One tends to search for a deeper meaning in life.
That one's life may be cut short should make no difference.
Life is such a blink of the eye in time.
When one part of you is sick, the sickness is felt by the other parts.
What affects one, affects all.
You can be working a math problem or be participating in sports.
If you do not follow correct basic procedures,
The outcome will determine whether the solution is right or wrong.
Whether you win or lose.
The results determine the effect on the team,
The outcome of the event, and the attitude of the individuals.
The whole is no better than its parts.
What you give out, you get back in proportion to that amount.

This goes for your spiritual man.
The whole is no better than its parts.
Laws in society must be enforced on all members equally,
To win the trust of those governed.
Otherwise, you will have dissention and mistrust.
The whole is no better than its parts.

In the natural realm, breed a horse with a mule, you get a jackass.
Breed a male with a female, you reproduce a male or female.
There is a natural order in life for regeneration,
When the laws of God are followed.
If not followed, there will be degeneration.
And a dying out of the particular species…
Spiritually reborn, we must strive to be like Jesus, to attain the
higher goodness.

Otherwise, you stand the chance of being turned over to a
reprobate mind.
Thinking what is wrong in the world is the right thing to do.
Your heart becomes hardened to the things of God.
When this worldly life has ended, you stand a chance of being lost
forever,
Because you rejected the whole of which we are a part.

THE BEST DAY

The best day is today.
Not because of what you received, but what you gave away.
Your day should not be measured as to how long,
But you attitude in fixing what is wrong.
When you start the morning after getting a good nights rest,
Remember to give thanks to God, for you he has truly blessed.
The Lord began your morning by opening you eyes,
So that you can marvel at his fascinating sky.
As you continue to gaze and look around,
Your mind is amazed at what the Lord brings forth from the ground.
Each day is different from the other,
The way a sister is different from her brother.
As children of God, and Sons of the Way,
Thank you Lord; the best day is today.

MONEY

Money is good, and it is wealth.
People seek it, to the detriment of health.
Money should not precede righteous thoughts.
If done, with money you can be bought.
Money like most exchange is a tool.
Number one in life, it's the rule of the fool.
Ultimate power is righteous use of mind.
Money guided by love focuses on all mankind.
Money is necessary for food, clothing and rent.
It is also used to run branches of government.
Misused money by government caused inflation.
This is why America is an indebted nation.
The richly rich have put money first.
This has taken away from human worth.
We no longer look at our brother's plight.
For us, love of money determines who's right.

WOMAN

She puts up with hardship and pain.
Her beauty matches her brain.
She is a woman.

She carries herself with pride.
She is the apple of her husband's eye.
She is a woman.

She is responsible for birth.
When hurt, she will be there first.
She is a woman.

She is always full of grace.
She brings joy to a child's face.
She is a woman.

Her love is of warmth and charm.
To her husband her love stays strong.
She is a woman.

A woman of value.

MY DAUGHTER, HIS WIFE

My daughter is no longer a little girl.
Now, married, life is one which she must share.
She's the pride of her father, her mother's daughter.
Her husband, their children will call father.

On her wedding day, she had such a lovely gown;
Upon her head stood a majestic crown.
She strolled down the aisle with her dad at her side,
There was a sense of loss as her mother cried.

Her knowledge was I have to let you go.
You will always remain a part of my soul
Her husband to be was full of pride,
As our daughter walked up the steps to be at his side.

If they only knew it was from God
This marriage was birthed,
They will have to please God
For this marriage to gain worth.
Material things will not be worth a dime.
Unless, for each other, they make time.

God gives and God taketh away.
As husband and wife they must find time to play.
You will have life problems from day to day,
But things will work out if you have faith and pray,
Together, that is.
Don't say, "I am the man, I want it this way."
Remember to have compassion,
Understanding and love day after day.

Don't say, "I am a woman; I do as I please"
Remember in getting along, that you must remain at ease.
To be a friend, you must be friendly,
To be loved, you must give love.

Give and it will be given back to you.
Nothing happens on its own.
Just look to Jesus and your house will be a happy home.
Peace be with you as your marriage evolves.

DOUBLE MINDED

Black woman, Black woman
Don't complain
Black woman, Black woman
Support your man
Black woman, Black woman
Let me in (knock, knock)
Black woman, Black woman
I'll give you my love and be your friend
Black woman, Black woman
Do your part
Black woman, Black woman
Show a loving heart
Black woman, Black woman
Don't be hurt
Black woman, Black woman
When you were sick, I became your nurse
Black woman, Black woman
You say he's rough
Black woman, Black woman
It's you who is acting tough
Black woman, Black woman
You are, oh, so tender
Black woman, Black woman
Your ways are such a mixture, like food in a blender
Black woman, Black woman
You say he's lazy
Black woman, Black woman
Why do you have his baby?
Black woman, Black woman
I know I act crazy
Black woman, Black woman
I am in love; will you have my baby?
Black woman, Black woman
Share the blame
Black woman, Black woman

Treat him right and he'll do the same
Black woman, Black woman
At times I don't give a damn
Black woman, Black woman
You are driving me insane
Black woman, Black woman
I think I've said enough
Black woman, Black woman
Don't forget you are my stuff
Oh! But the wrath to come.
I am just having fun! Hint! Hint!

A CRY FROM THE GRAVE

(Mother, Abortioner, and Abortionist)

I gave life.
And you took it away.
Woe to you, You must pay.
I gave it to you.
To keep for while.
But oh! How it hurt me,
You destroyed my child.
You should have hearkened to my voice,
Life of a child was my choice.
Ways of the world aren't mine.
Study the scripture.
My ways are divine.
My word tells of the good news.
In the end you will pay your dues.
My ways are high above your ways.
And will be until the end of day.
I won't come down.
For your deeds you will be eternally bound.
I said in my word.
You were bought with a price.
It's not yours to take a life.
With the cut of a knife.
The child was given to you to raise.
Your mind was on earthly praise.
This is my body; I do as I please.
In the end, you will be brought to your knees.
All things begin with me, and all things will end.
The killing of the unborn the worst of sin.
The harm you did to the least of these little ones you will pay.
I'll bring to remembrance on judgement day.
When you took an innocent life, for a price.
Every deed you have done is written in the book.
This deed caused the angels in heaven to cry as they looked.

But who are you to make that determination. I made you!
If you obey my word you would take care of what I made.
And I would deliver you as my words have said.
Get your mind out of the way.
And you will see my glory each and every day.
Not just one,
But as often as you let my will be done.

GONE IN THE FLESH, ALIVE IN THE SPIRIT

As I slept at my departed mother's home,
Her peaceful spirit penetrated each room.
She may have left in physical form,
The love she left in the spirit is still strong.
While living, she got on her knees to pray
That the Lord watch over her children and
Individuals she came in contact with day after day.
As she got older, she had doubts and felt insecure,
But the love she gave her children when they were young kept them near.
Her children live close, some live far away.
This matriarch of a woman was the main character in this family play.
She gave, she gave, and she kept on giving.
Her greatest joy was fellowship in Christian living.
Mother is a woman who is surely missed.
Her life in Christ kept up from the pits,
The pits of hell that is.

STAIR, STEPS AND CHILDREN

Stairs with steps remind me of a child making his first steps in life.
A step must be made properly in order to advance.
If a step of a child is too short or too long he may fall.
Each proper step forward is looked at as a victory.
He gains courage and boldness with each proper step to continue the walk.
Moving forward is the only way to see what life has to offer on the other side of the hill.
If you look behind, you may stumble or fall.
You must never give up.
Your journey may become stagnant or cause you to stymie the process of growth.
In the process of life you move forward or you will be left behind.
Steps are like life.
You move forward or you will be left behind.
Steps are like life.
There is a beginning and there is an end.
Therefore make steps that are steady, timely and ongoing or you will fall behind.

HER BEAUTY PROVOKES MY LOVE

Her hair was wavy and black; it danced on her head like the mane of a lion running at full speed, flowing below the nape of her neck to the back, with intriguing strains of gray. It sheened as the sunlight hovered over her head during the day. This hair had such a splendid mixture, which embraced a refined texture.

The gentle smile and her trembling hands let me know she feels secure in my warm embrace as we dutifully whisper words that provoke music to the ears and medicine to the heart, cleansing the soul of impurities. A fiery passion infiltrates my heart as her face displays the gentleness of a mother after the birth of her child…full with calm, innocence and peace.

The curvatures of her shoulders were supremely beautiful as they punctuated a perfectly symmetrical neck. As her hair escaped toward her tiny waist, her silk skirt took on a sensuous shape. Her eyes and eyelids reminded me of a full moon on a cloudy night. As the clouds disappear, the moon can be fully visible and its brightness shine forth.

As I kissed her eyelids and gave them a gentle caress, her eyes opened widely as though looking into the world of the loved one whose spirit and intensity revealed her passion. The flaming heat of passion incited her nostrils and they flared up like a filly during a spring morning, full of life and a keen awareness of anything that moved. Her lips appeared full and succulently vibrant. As I meditated upon the dangling jewels protruding from her ears. Her movement was profound.

The enhancing movement of her hips gave a pulsating overture with each enticing stride of her lovely legs, so shapely and long as she made each step over the ground. She walks with a strident grace as she travels from place to place. She displayed a feminine muscular tone. She showed a very high energy level, as she moved with the grace of a leaping gazelle. As reflected in her stride, her demeanor was one of pride as witnessed by the sparkle in her eye. To hear her voice is to hear a harp playing a beautiful melody by a mountain stream, each word having its own texture and thrill. The beauty of words from her lips cast no doubt, this lady was as refined as a cultured pearl.

Yes, her precious love was like the beginning of spring, alive with youth and activity, full of newness. It awakened in me naughty energy and desires that were dormant but are now tacitly tingling the nerve ending of my heart and my thoughts, causing my eyes to contract and become hazed with glaze. It was not only her physical beauty but also the beauty of her giving her love without reservation and trusting me to be the caretaker of her spiritual awakening.

But oh! If I could love you the way I love you, you would have no doubt of my love. To love you is to use seduction without being reluctant. Our love is so precious when we give and receive, thereby forming an eternal bond in which the heaven we look forward to going to when we leave this world can be had here on earth. This is the provoking I look forward to each time we commune together.

RUNNERS TAKE YOUR MARK

Runners are men and women who are sane.
Running from the heart, they put up with pain.
Some like races long, some like races short.
Each step in the end determines who got the biggest heart.
Most runners start out slow, other start out fast.
They give it their all without running out of gas.
Some runners are large, some runners are small.
They move to the line when the starter calls.
Runners move forward like a wave in the ocean.
When the gun goes off, they are poetry in motion.
Women are competitive as the men.
They fight their adversary to the very end.
Competitors start races with strong legs and strong minds.
At the end, they are contented just to better their time.
The winner feels like king of the hill for a while.

MY BEDROOM

In the bedroom I love to sit.
I go there to get my spirit enriched.
My bedroom is where I go to dream.
I meditate in my heart what life means.
My bedroom is sunshine in the rain.
It is there I think, plot and plan.
My bedroom is where I go to be alone.
It is the place my house feels like a home.
My bedroom is full of lights and love.
It is where I received confidence from above.
In my bedroom I hold my wife in my arms.
It is also the place I feel like a king on a throne.
My bedroom is where I go to sleep.
It is where I find the greatest peace.

HAPPY AND EMOTIONAL WOMAN

Woman sang
Woman dance
Woman seeks and finds romance

Woman jump
Woman shout
Woman live to get a spouse

Woman holler
Woman cry
Woman in love full of pride

Woman rant
Woman rave
Woman happy throughout her days

All things are possible.

MY BROTHER

I have a brother named Glenn.
He cared for mother to the end.
The day she died, her children cried.
He stayed close to her side, a man of pride.
While looking intuitively into her face.
His thoughts were she's gone to a greater place.
There we are told the streets are paved with gold.
She will have continual joy springing from her soul.
In this world he would put her to bed at night.
Remembering, she took care of him in this life.
They had a love from the cradle to the grave.
This was a love from heaven that only God gave.

HURT

Never say something that can hurt another.
In truth these are your sisters and brothers.
They may not be of your daddy's seed or mother's flesh.
But they are children of God and that's the test.
Too often we judge people by the color of skin.
Through spiritual eyes this is a great sin
It is a shame we associate in terms of color.
Yet it was Jesus who died for all his brothers.
We humans harp, mourn, and throw sticks and stones.
Instead of being first to invite our neighbors home.
Yes we do love, we love in part.
Forgetting, true love must come from the heart.

I DREAM OF GENIE

On this moon lit night, as the moon was full and the stars appeared to run across the sky, I dreamed of Genie, as she bathed in milk and honey. Instead of drying off with a towel my thoughts were to lick the sweetness which was beginning to slowly drip from the top of her head down to her feet. I would then massage the honey into her shoulders as I lap the flow of honey from her ear lobes. I then intruded to siphon the sweet nectar that had been massaged into her shoulder as she began to relax. I turned her on her back to lavish and ravage her with gentle kisses and raucous romance, as she captured me with her looks and caressed me with her smile, as she voiced words of wisdom that gave warmth to my touch and inflamed my heart. As our lips slowly pressed tightly to each other, our tongues touched in passing. The tip of my tongue reached for the warmth coming from the roof of her mouth, which gave off a salivary strawberry scent. It caused electrified charges to emit from my heart and an impulsive uplifting of my arms that stimulated me to shiver and shake as I reached for the ceiling. She then thrust her arms up and around my neck in a passionate and soothing manner. Oh! The comfort of my feelings and emotions she generated, as my heart was sensuously entrapped by the potency of her feminine sensuality.

She was a treasure chest of love filled to the top with life and a zest for living, yet mysterious enough to the point where you could never completely know her, but you were consumed in trying to figure her out. She was a figure of fitness with fluid motion in her every movement yet she stayed focused in satisfying my intense urges as I sulked in her pristine beauty. I gravitated toward her smile. She has such a beautiful smile along with dimples in her jaws that punctuated her charming face. Her young girl giddiness and laughter was like that of a teenager causing her embarrassment but her statuesque shape was that of a fully voluptuous lady who knew that her presence exposed her well developed endowments. The more we talked to each other, the more we communicated our thoughts and feelings, our hopes and dreams. We had a strong physical attraction that in the beginning was never expressed in words. The induced attraction caused by our closeness gave a wealth of information of our future attachment to each other, as I experienced the nail tips of her fingers digging deeply into the fleshly part of my shoulder blades. I could feel the tenseness of her arms tighten with an explosive gripping. Holding on as if the next intake of breath depended on her being able to have a sigh of relief. Yet she wallowed in the warmth of my love, slithering to her knees like a snake stalking its prey, slow and totally aware, and with obedient compliance showing.

Her love was innocent and trustworthy and yet she wanted me to know that it is given with all the freedom that is within her. The fulfillment for love could be seen in her eyes as her eyes became alive with a depth that mirrored her soul, as floating on a cloud like a feather when dropped from a mountain through the air, down and around, at times up and then softly descending, touching the ground. Her pupils became so large that you knew she was able to absorb all that they could grasp. Her love was from the heart, devoid of whether she may get hurt. It harbored no second thoughts as to where it might lead. She had many sorrows in her life but she never complained as she nurtured a strong will to live day after day and not giving in to doubt and fears as she feverishly sought advancement to a better life.

What a delight to see the warmth of her face shine like the sun and lips that were full and succulent to the palate when taste were like a full course meal with all the trimmings and dripping with delight.

Her children, which were three and five, were her life force. They could be counted on to give her emotional drive and support. The more she saw their need for her, the more drive and determination surfaced from her being.

She moaned the words, "I love you," I reciprocated. Whether she meant it at the moment or for a season, they were strongly spoken in the present to give thanks to the heightened ecstasy she was again anticipating, then I awoke, looked around to discover Oh! What a dream.

LIFE GIVER

It begins in the spirit.
It becomes the word.
It is a gift.
It came from above.
It started in love.
It is life.
Created by the one who is our maker.
The beginning of all things and is our savior.
He created the first man, Adam, from the dust.
And in him, he put trust.
Adam fell, and put the blame on Eve.
And since that time mankind has been deceived.
God had given them dominance over the whole world.
Since their sin in the garden, we have had nothing but turmoil.
God had given them knowledge of right and wrong,
But they decided to listen to another song.
Now the life we have is in the Son.

IN YOUR FACE

Looking through the mirror.
I like what I see.
Looking through the mirror.
I see a reflection of me.
Looking through the mirror.
Can really be a pain.
If you feel what is reflected back,
Is truly not the man.
What stands in front of the mirror.
Must be seen through your eyes.
Because when you stand before the mirror,
It will reflect if you have pride.
When you stand before the mirror.
You have a mind set.
That in looking through the mirror,
You will look your very best.
When you look at yourself in the mirror.
Make sure you are contented.
If the mirror falls off the wall,
You will probably be offended.

ALL ON THE GOODFOOT

He could jump up
Spin around
Come down
Do the splits
Come out of his bag
With a brand new trick
All on the goodfoot.

JB could scream and holler
With distinctive authoritative power
Bedazzling your mind
And losing no time
As he slide and guide
All on the goodfoot.

He could shift gears and shake
Throw the mike from hand to hand
Thinking, as around he'd twirl
This is a man's world
All on the goodfoot.

JB would twist and shout
Leaving no doubt
He was the Godfather of soul
They sent him to prison
From there he's arisen
Bigger and better than before
As his fans ask for more
From the Godfather of soul
All on the goodfoot.

THE FIRST LOVE

Love is giving and it causes growth.
Growth increases your gain.
The gain is a fulfillment of God's plan.
Love is to the spirit what God is to man.
He laid the burden on Jesus to complete the plan.
Jesus didn't give in and he didn't give up.
He just sup with the disciples,
And drank from the cup,
The disciples didn't understand.
When he ascended to the Father,
He appeared to their spirit as being,
More than just a man.
The disciples meditated long,
And they meditated hard.
Then they realized my God! My God!
You've given the first love.

REFLECTION

Modern living is like a race.
You hurry to get to the finish.
Once there you have to start.
All over again.
You repeat this procedure over and over.
You wonder what have I accomplished?
Is this all there is to life?
Finally, you realize,
The most important ingredient is left out.
God, His Son, and the denying of self.
Once these three are included,
Life becomes a joy.
You savor the wind as it blows through your nostrils.
You look at nature and taste it.
Enjoying the beauty of flowers, birds singing,
Roses springing.
You vividly remember the past,
And combine it with the present to develop a better future.
You become sensitive.
You release the tension and pressures of life and turn from poor
health to good health.
Your mind and your body relax as if you were at play.
So that you can enjoy another day.
You realize you must live a life of love.
Understand your fellow man.
And in doing so your whole life changes.
For the better that is.

GOD CREATED

The God I serve, by his word, created the heavens,
And all that is beneath it.
Satan, as the ruler of this world,
Uses lies, deceit, and craftiness to abate this.
Jesus, the Son of God, was then sent into the world to redeem man.
He is the life-giving blood that fulfilled God's earthly plan.
Satan, with his imps and demons,
All cast from above,
Could not fathom the overwhelming favor,
That we have in God's love.

HAVE A HEART

Here is a rose that has never died,
But will always live.
It was fashioned with hands that love,
And is an expression of hands that give.
It comes from the earth.
From my spirit it was birthed.
You see it physically,
But it first existed spiritually.
It is love expressed openly.
It is meant to be felt emotionally.
I do not see you from day to day.
My words cannot express,
What my heart wants to say.
In life giving people want to live.
I think and feel it so much
A wonderful expression.
When love in you shows you have a heart to give.

HAVE A GOOD DAY

May your day begin like the sunrise.
Effortlessly, peaceful, and bright so that the world can see.
Giving life and inspiration, yet putting all who witness it in awe
and at ease.
As night follows day.
We never fathom the importance of how the sun's magnetic pull on
the earth has its way.
We must remember that life has a reason.
And that we are put here for a season.
Our lives can be long and sometimes short.
The role we play is a very important part.
Days, at times, may be hard.
The experience we receive from our maker should make us
applaud.
The thoughts we receive throughout the day.
Should be emblazoned on our conscience as we kneel and pray.
May the air you breathe and the thoughts you think,
Make you feel special each day as you give thanks.

I AM AFRAID

Don't be afraid.
I am like you.
Don't be afraid.
I have fear too.
When we are afraid,
We can't relate.
If we aren't afraid,
Companions we can make.
As we look towards each other,
We realize we both have a mother.
Commonality in us abounds.
As we look at each other up and down,
Sitting face to face in a chair.
We see a sameness that we share.

Afraid! I am not afraid.

FEAR

Fear is a quality found in man.
It causes him grief and the severest of pain.
It can come into your life for no reason.
And sever your thinking for many a season.
Fear can tinker with your emotions.
Destroying your self-confidence and strong devotion.
Fear can cause you to develop a frivolous state.
And without objective thinking, you lose your mate.
Fear cuts off oxygen to your brain.
Thoughts are so mingled you feel less than a man.
Fear has broken many relationships and lives,
Causing love to disappear between husbands and wives.
When you feel you have reached the bottom of the pit and been
deceived,
Look to Jesus and he will fill your every need.

NATURAL BIRTH

Into this world I came,
Due to the love of a woman for a man.

Out of my mother's womb I was birthed.
With patience and love, I gained worth.

My mother at no time cried, showed anguish or pain,
As she raised me from a child to a young man.

The early days of my life, I was talked to, disciplined, and loved,
As my mother received spiritual guidance from above.

She never let me forget that from God I was given.
God gave me to her as a gift from heaven.

CHILDREN

Children are a work of art.
In innocence they are brought forth.
Through expressions of love most children are born.
They are first nourished in their mother's womb until they are
strong.
Leaving the world of the secure womb the child is brought to a
place called home.
The healthy child and the healthy home go hand in hand.
This is the way it must be in God's plan.
The home must have an environment that nourishes the body,
mind, and spirit as one.
To the child, life will be thought of as fun.
Instruction from parents to the children will seem like an equation,
Because of the children's need for gentle persuasion.

WIND

Where does it come from? No one knows.
Where does it go? No one knows.
It can be quiet.
It can be a blast.
It can throw objects far and fast.
It can be a violent cyclonic force, fierce within.
By another name this would be called a hurricane.
It is noted for making leaps and bounds,
Sometimes causing destruction of small towns.
In open spaces you can see this funnel,
As it engulfs objects into its tunnel.
Indians of old called it the spirit wind.
It moved about seeking and searching for sinful men.
After it has run its course,
People in its path feel remorse.
They look around and search deep within,
And come to the conclusion, it began as the wind.

THE BOXER

Boxers learn from an early age,
Being in a ring is like a play; you're on stage,
You must practice very hard to make the grade.

Boxers are men, who train with disdain,
Putting up with agony, punishment, and pain,
To be the very best and find out who is the better man.

True warriors become physically and mentally tough.
One of these attributes is not enough,
To deter your opponent and convince him you have heart.

Boxers train each day without a mumble.
Planning, plotting, and moving like a ballerina or a lion in the
jungle.
So they are sharp in combat, when they rumble.

Boxing to some seems to be the sport of the unknowledged.
These athletes are of long, medium, and short sizes.
A few boxers have degrees from college.

The sport of boxing has been said to be,
For those of the ghetto in order to make money
To afford to enter school for higher learning.

Yes! it has helped them get discipline.
So that they don't turn to robbing.
But become better men.

THE GREATEST BOXER EVER LIVED

(A Tribute to Sugar Ray Robinson)

Sugar Ray. He was a glamorous man.
Had lethal punching power in both hands.
He exhibited true sportsmanship, in and out of the ring,
Especially in combat doing his thing.
Ray had energy, stamina, and pep.
Boxing was what he's most adept
He made economic and financial gain.
Just having fame was not worth a damn.
Refused to let trainers and managers control his cash.
Many fighters did and had nothing after boxing had passed.
His foot movement, poetry in motion, Oh! So sweet.
You'd become mesmerized and get up out of your seat.
Ray was to boxing what the Drifters and the Spinners were to
music: A classic.
He could use individual hands to triple hook and double right.
Then comes in underneath and end the fight.
Man what a whammer!
He'd seduce his opponents with his hammer (left hook that is).
Ray was the greatest pound for pound.
Could knock you out in any round.
Fought intelligently and didn't clown.
His punches came like bullets in a machine gun.
You would find yourself always on the run,
Not knowing which punch is the bomb that knocked you out.
In the 40's Ray and Joe Louis gave the Black people inspiration.
We didn't have true upward mobility in America, our true nation.
Ray was a man who could box, dance, and act.
In all that he did, he never forgot he was Black.
Joe Louis was great; Mohammed Ali was great and fast;
Anyone who saw Ray knew he was the true master of fisticuffs
present and past.

In memory of the Sugar Man
Best of the Best

THE GREATEST ATHLETE

He understands the who, what, when, where, and why of the game.
The greatest of athletes begins each season with a plan.
Whether well or hurt, he give 100% of himself each second,
minute, play of the season.
Knowing winning has great value when you incorporated the
ability to reason.
The greatest athlete pushes himself harder to be in the best shape.
And using his mind in making the best use of his time.
A true measure of the greatest test,
Is if his striving has made him the best.
The greatest athlete has persistence and drive.
His vision and mental faculties are focused on the prize.
Paying attention to detail is honed to perfection.
As he analyzes his performance he can find no objection.
He has the greatest love one can have for what he is doing.
That is giving his all and if death comes in the process of the game,
it is his choosing.

WHO'S TO BLAME?

Street smart and ghetto slick.
Violent thugs carry Uzi's to get their kicks.
Killing their brother just for a fix.

They use these guns to build up their esteem.
Treating their adversary very mean.
They travel the city with ghetto blasters.
To those who use drugs, he is master.

Some call themselves angels,
Angels of death.
For their violence,
Mothers wept.

They are filled with violence and pain.
The way of saying I am a man.
Ruling through marijuana and cocaine.

Short name for cocaine is coke.
For marijuana it is Mary Jane or grass.
After using it, you have an acute sense of the past.

Mainly controlled by drug lords,
And used by straights, prostitutes, and pimps,
Also by wimps and limps.

Those who use them will never be the same.
Because they are now controlled by the "man" supplier

But all isn't lost if you want to change.
Look to Jesus and he'll revamp your plan.
With Jesus it is never too late.
If you desire to change your fate.

You are guaranteed you won't be the same.

Your change will cause you to be a renewed man.

Conclusion of the whole matter; fear God and keep his
commandments,
For this is the whole duty of man.
For God shall bring every work into judgement with every secret
thing,
Whether it be good or whether it be evil.

IT'S IN THE EYES

Eyes come in all sizes and shapes.
But certain eyes capture your mate.
Her eyes were dark brown surrounded by the purest white.
Encased in sockets that were perfectly round.
And a perfectly oval face of burnt sienna brown.
The expressiveness of her eyes ran very deep.
That could cause hesitance in a man's voice as he speaks.
The white and the brown of her eyes had a glisten.
When you looked into her eyes as she spoke, you would listen.
Her eyes were set evenly apart.
With lashes long and dark.
Her face an object of beauty.
Yet she didn't act as a cutie.
She had a smile unblemished and a beauty that's raw.
That unleashed the radiance of her curvaceous jaw.
She could look at you in a fashion,
That could entice you into a whirlwind of passion.
There was a covetness in her to establish; she was no faker;
For she truly cherished her maker.
Her eyes revealed that her soul was sealed.
She never told anyone, her eyes revealed it.

WHO IS SHE?

She could never see things in black and white.
There were always shades of gray in between.
Her objectivity was never balanced,
If you understand what I mean.
She may say yes, she may say no,
But never concludes the matter.
Her answer was such and you didn't get very much.
She would insist you gave her improper data.

WHY DO I LOVE YOU?

I love you.
Because you want to be loved.
I love you.
Because you chose me to receive your love.
I love you.
Because your giving of self causes me to reciprocate,
Thereby causing me to contemplate and anticipate.
I love you when you smile.
Because it shows the warmth and beauty of your soul.
It reflects your vulnerability, yet I want to be there to be your
strength.
I love you when you laugh.
Because of the joy that comes from your heart,
And in me it sets a spark.
I love you when you hurt, I want to absorb the pain, and give you
comfort.
Your love causes me to drop my defenses and have confidence in
you.
With you I can let go and let my love flow.
Your love is a pleasure that can't be measured.
I can suffer the hurt to the degree that I can pick myself up; to be
uninhibited.
Your love is like a ripe peach with furs. Oh! So soft.
As it is stroked, its furs lie down so gently and spring up intensely.
I love you.
Because I know your needs.
A hug around your waist lets you know you are safe,
United as one to enjoy life's privileged fun.
A kiss to your eyes lets you know you are prized.
As I fathom the beauty of your soul through your eyes.
A squeeze to your hand lets you know I am your man.
It secures my love for, and to, you.
A kiss on your lips can soften your trip.
As we travel life's lonely path together.
A kind word in time as a gift from your mind.

A soft kind word to eliminate wrath.
Although there may be many trials along life's way,
We always remember there must be time for play.
You are my dream, my love, sent from above.
One of a kind who enraptures my mind and causes me to see stars.

This is why I love you.

GENTLENESS

Some people think gentleness is a fault.
But do you know gentleness can melt the hardest of hearts?

Gentleness has a way of diffusing anger.
And making friends of total strangers.

Gentleness is a quality that can't be bought.
When applied with friendliness, can appeal to a woman's heart.

Hey! Don't take life so serious.
Try a little gentleness.

I CAN

I can be the friend.
Who is there to the very end.
I can be a clown.
Who brings you a smile, when you want to frown.
I can lift you from darkness and despair.
At moments when you are angry, and want to pull out your hair.
I can be a lover.
Who is closer than your mother.
All these I can be, to renew your feeling.
If you look to God, he will give you spiritual healing.

HE IS MY BROTHER

He was the first son of my father,
Proud son of my mother.
The first child to be born,
First child in our home.
He is my brother.

He was inquisitive and strong.
A quiet and silent baby who hardly cried.
Maybe it was because he had a lot of pride.
He is my brother.

Mother dedicated him to the Lord.
His purpose for being born!
To fulfill God's cause.
He is my brother.

My brother led by example.
He refused to be pampered.
During school days he strived and struggled to succeed,
Giving his best made him feel pleased.
He is my brother.

He lives life with enthusiasm to its best.
Today he is a man of success.
He is my brother.

TOGETHERNESS

Clay was a man with a plan.
He sought and won Zane's hand.
I played cupid and brought her flowers.
To Zane, Clay was the man of the hour.
Zane and Clay had commitment.
Their marriage was one of enrichment.
To him, she was the rarest.
He loved and treated her in all fairness.
Behind him she would always stand.
For her, Clay was her perfect man.
Through thick and thin, he could depend.
She'd be there to the very end.
She would stand by her man.
No one knows who treated the other better,
For they stuck together through life's stormy weather.
Zane had confidence in her man.
They built a business that now stands.
As she gave Clay free rein and a hand.
With business skills honed to perfection,
Customer and associate have found no objection.
When you need printing, Clay's printing is your best selection.
My pen was taken in hand.
To enlighten you of the story of
Clay and Zane.

HOME

My mother was a woman virtuous and kind.
Who gave love to her children during the hardest of time.
To her children and her friends, she was always caring.
At no time did she act over bearing.
Problems arose that would irk the best.
This woman called mom would stand the test.
Dad was a man who worked night and day.
In order that we'd have food and a place to stay.
When he was not working on his job, he was working at home,
Making sure that his children knew right from wrong.

LONELINESS

You can be in a crowd and be alone.
You can be with the one you love and be alone.
When your soul is restless you can feel along,
But when you call on you maker and let all of life's worries go,
You can be alone and have peace.
Go into the inner chambers of your mind and pray.
You will witness a presence that will brighten up your day.
Being alone can be a blessing; being alone can be a curse,
But the power is in your hand to give loneliness worth.
Loneliness is a state of mind.

HE CARES

When no one else is there, he'll be there.
When you are down, he'll pick you up.
When you have time, he'll show you a sign.
When you feel like you can no longer carry on,
He'll give you strength to your spirit to make you strong.
He'll give you love, hope, and knowledge.
He'll provide you with the things you won't find in college.
He'll provide you with standards that the average man cannot
measure.
If you continue to look to him, he'll implant on your mind his
truths and his treasures.
All that he gives you won't come cheap.
Until you deny yourself and profess Jesus is Lord, and bow at his
feet.

LOVE IS LIGHT

Love is like a window; the wider you open the window, the more
light enters.
The least glimmer of light gives hope,
And when you swallow, you feel a lump in your throat.
The smallest crack in the window brings love to your world,
Making you feel like the rarest of pearls.
Love begins in our thoughts,
Thereby provoking emotional feeling in our heart.
The more you open your heart,
The more you are capable of bringing forth.
The more love you receive, the more vulnerable you become.
The more vulnerable you become, the least you want to be one.
As love penetrates you through and through,
You look forward to being united as two.
Our hearts may palpitate, skip a beat and cause us to beam.
For love to continue, we must use our imagination and dreams.
Love is the light that you let in,
The more you give of yourself,
The more your heart wants to bend.

AGAIN

A relationship between a man and a woman
Must be built on trust.
Otherwise there's continual fuss.
Paying a higher cost don't make you the boss.
You will end up losing your horse.
Learn to control your mouth.
Uncontrolled you'll lose your clout.
If not receiving
Check out your actions,
They may be deceiving.
Home should be a place that is warm.
Not a place that is torn
Your mate now wants to roam.
Home has become a thorn.
Giving of sad moans and vicious groans.
Check yourself, if you begin to doubt.
Think you got the upper hand?
You are about to lose your man?
He now doesn't give a damn.
Things still the same?
You thought you were the boss?
Think you have the arrow that keeps him over the barrel?
Your thinking is narrow.
Check out your behavior; depend on your savior.
He should be your boss and leader,
He is no cheater.
Be careful with your thoughts, you can lose your heart.
You thought you were the boss.

UNFORESEEN VIOLENCE

In departing from my home.
I crossed the bridge of Bayou St. John.
The grass on the ground had its morning frost,
As I approached the lights of a 4-way cross.

While walking through a city park,
I decided to sit upon a log.
As I sat and looked into the sky,
Upon my tennis shoe lit a Dragonfly.

As kids we called them Mosquito Hawk or Dragonfly,
The violence in them we were never taught.
Whether called Mosquito Hawk or Dragonfly,
They will attack another until one dies.

I looked at one that landed on my tennis shoe,
Along came others attached at two.
I thought they were mating, which was not the case,
The one that was on top devoured the other's head and face.

What a terrible, terrible sight.
As the one on the bottom flaps its wings to get loose,
From jaws like a vice,
I had never in person seen such violence in the insect world.
This behavior caused my stomach to curl.

This was just a prelude to the violence in man,
Whose instinct toward one another inflicts,
The very such pain.

If we would only follow the righteous teaching of our Maker,
We would refuse to be violent partakers.
As partakers of good and followers of the light,
The foundation that Jesus laid would instill in us to do right.

DAMAGE FROM WITHIN

Have you ever seen a luscious green tree?
It has a beautiful outward appearance,
As far as the eye can see.
Yet beneath the bark and far within,
The membrane of the tree can be very thin.
We can see the insects and pests on leaves.
Another creature is working destruction that can topple whole
trees.
These insects have wings to fly, mouths to bite.
They are called termites.
They are capable of destroying villages.
They are capable of destroying towns.
They have wiped houses off their foundations, no longer to be
considered home.

THE CLEVEREST MAN

The cleverest man will never worry.
He thinks things through and never says "Sorry."
Cleverness is just another word for smart.
This individual puts his ideas on paper when he starts.
He never has to exercise his authority through power or might.
Due to innate cleverness, he thinks he's right.
He never mixes wisdom with folly.
This takes away from the truthfulness of knowledge.
The clever man puts his thoughts down in a logical sequence,
When another reads it, it stands out like a lighthouse beacon.
The clever man has a positive outlook and is always learning.
With this precious quality, Jesus in his heart, he's always yearning.

MY LOVE

My love can give you strength since it is true
and from the heart.
My love can make your perception of objects clear
and ripen your thoughts.
My love can pick you up when you are down.
My love can bring a smile to your face instead
of a frown.
My love place no limit or boundaries on or
around its borders.
My love is given freely without establishing a quota.
My love creates that which is not visibly seen.
My love produces creativity and pleasant dreams.
My love can produce positive energy for the good of mankind.
My love is such that you lose the existence of time.
My love can cause you to forget the negative
that limits you and stunts your growth.
My love can also seem like a dream and
you refuse to be awoke.
Because reality may cause it to escape from you.
My love makes you think.

CHILDREN GONE, DADDY STILL HOME

When he asked you, do you love me?
You'd say can't you see I am still here.
All he wanted to hear from you was, I love you dear.
In the past you put the children first.
Yet, you always was the one who ended up hurt.
The children are grown now and gone.
No longer do they have interest in coming home.
You put all your energy into those boys,
Their attention is now focused on the lady of their choice.
Remember the man you chose first that day.
You see he 's the only one to stay.
Dad continually showed his love for you through thick and thin,
First place of your love for him should be to the very end.
He never forgot for better or worse for rich or poor.
Yet Dad showed his strength by not walking out the door.

Did you forget your first love?

WHEN MY WIFE CRIES

My wife cries when she's hurt.
In my life, she wants to be first.

My wife cries when we argue over money.
My wife cries when I abstain from calling her honey.

My wire cries when I hoop, holler, and complain.
My wife cries when I am not a compassionate man.

My wife cries and says, "I can't take this anymore."
I cried when she packed up and walked out the door.

Now my wife left me crying, Why?

COVER UP

Most males who drank alcohol think it makes the man.
Once they become addicted it brings a lot of pain.

On women and children it has brought forth hurt,
Mom would always say, "children, we must give dad worth."

I have seen its destruction in my family at best,
we were torn apart seeking to find some rest.

Dad saying, "I won't do it again baby", was continually heard,
that got old when you find dad is not true to his word.

We did not want to lose him, he was all we had,
yet his drinking caused grief and made me sad.

In childhood his drinking brought out my worst fears,
to hear ambulance and police sirens, you thought he's no longer
here.

Under the influence I'd think he had an accident,
knowing that if he died, he'd be hell sent.

Drinking was a problem he needed to fix,
as a youngster, his drinking was making me sick.

Dad was told he must willfully seek the strength of the Lord.
His human nature would rebel and want to remain boss.

Life for him was a seesaw, sometimes up and then down,
without total allegiance to the Lord, he's no longer around.

TIME WILL TELL

When young, days seemed to never end.
As I get older, I cant' finish what I begin.
In enjoying what I do, time moves fast.
When having headaches, time just won't pass.
In my middle years, I had lots of tears.
As I reach old age, I inherit many fears.
When young, I put up with anguish and pain.
As old age crept in, is it worthy just to be a man?
The process of aging has finally taken its toll.
Now I am looking forward to being placed in a hole.
The last breath is taken; the door in now shut.
I no longer have to play the role of being tough.

EGOTISTICAL MAN

He wrote her a letter that would cause her heart to melt.
After he read it three times, he fell in love with self.

Although he was trying to convey his thoughts.
It was with his words he was caught.

His letter convinced him to get puffed up and inside feel vain.
Each time he read it looking in the mirror you saw a self centered
man.

He would fold his arms across his chest.
All who knew him saw a pathetic mess.

"Ain't I pretty, ain't I pretty?" he would holler.
Others told him what he wanted to hear, just for a dollar.

Here is a man who couldn't tell the forest from the trees,
But the love he had for himself was for sure, a disease.

Sucker, sucker, the people would say.
We're going to make you pay to have your way.

He would jump up and down and exercise his mind.
His behavior was like a monkey, swinging from a vine.

Oh! What a selfish jerk.
In facing reality, boy was he hurt.

The love he had for himself could never be explained.
For he wasted it on himself trying to be his own man.

SPECIAL

You may not be a bagel, you may not be a bun,
those who witness your presence say you are a special one.
They may look at you, yet cant' interpret your thoughts.
When they get to know you they appreciate the specialness of your
heart.
As Cupid pulls his bow to shoot his arrow and zing goes the string
just enjoy life and all those special things.
May your heart sing music and you have peace of mind.
I wish you all the special things that says you are attached to the
vine.

CAUSE I KNOW YOU

You moan, you groan, and you complain,
then you treat him as if he is not a man.
You do things without his consent,
he finds out and you become hell bent.

Your main weapon is between your legs,
you will use it to insure he is upstaged.
When he tells you about the action of your ways,
you become more determined to win your case

As you place the blame upon his shoulder;
he responds in a way you dislike, you act colder.
You can't see yourself but this is the way you are,
and this is the part that jacks up the brother's jaw.

I know you don't like what I have to say,
and since you don't, you won't be the leading lady in this play.
So get up off that thing, it will make you feel better.
I say, get up off that thing, and appreciate that treasure.

Get up off that thing, so I don't dis you.
Get up off that thing so later you won't have to say, I miss you.
Yes, you say I love you, but is it fair?
Your erratic behavior has me pulling out my hair.

UP JUMPED THE DEVIL

I was living life and feeling fine.
Up jumps the devil seeking to influence my mind.
All type of thoughts danced in my head.
Morning 'til night, they followed me to bed.
Satan continually throw arrows and darts,
my connection to the Lord ruled my heart.
At times my natural man was seeking to influence.
Through the spirit, the Lord increased my endurance.
Satan and his imps have proved to be clever,
everytime things are going right, up jumps the devil.

NEVER GIVE UP

Pursue, pursue, pursue, what you strive to do.
Never give up though at times things seemed tough.
When doubt intercedes in the recesses of your mind.
Correct all mistakes that affect your trying.
Whenever you find yourself being troubled,
expend more energy, your efforts, you double.
Always keep hope alive deep within.
And
Your desire to finish what you begin.

YOUR DOG

He barks, he howls.
He give me that facial scowl.

I am so scared, he makes me want to run.
Yet, you, the dog owner, take it as intended pun.

Your dog, he charges me and I do a little dance.
When his antics are over, I've wet in my pants.

You say your dog, he is oh so smart,
after you leave the scene, he seeks my every part.

Your words are ringing in my ears, he is very nice.
After he has bitten me, you have to pay the price.

The price for having him now, bring you pain.
You realize he can't be trusted around the Mailman.

Oh, that dog the price he made you pay!
As I sit upon my porch enjoying life from day to day,

You say that #* damn dog. Uh huh!

MARRIAGE

Marriage should never be looked at as a trap,
if done so, your energies will be sapped.

You will be like a man in prison,
bound and gagged by the world schism.

Good marriages are determined right from the start.
When problems arise just show a loving heart.

In truth, good marriages are determined by choice of selection,
that the rest of your married life, won't be one of objection.

Marriage is a continual test,
as you struggle to give your mate the best and no less.

THE CHURCH

The church should never be
looked at as a battleground where
members fight and fuss.

But a place of love that at
sometimes appears tough.

To often leaders act at the
hearing of others word.

Instead of having patience and
their comments deferred.

The purpose of the church is to
lift up the One True God.

If this is not the case, the church
will be seen as hypocritical and filled
with fraud.

The church should be a place of love and
tender-heartedness given in kind.

Where preaching of the word
can be a filter of the mind.

The preaching should remove impurities and
break down the crud.

Thus causing the church
followers to leave with a handshake
and some love.

THERE MUST BE A BALANCE

Good marital relationship is likened to a scale, in order to have a
proper
reading, there bust be a balance weight.
If one side of the scale is off center, there will be an incorrect
reading.
In a marital relationship, hurt feeling and emotions can cause
improper
readings of your mate.
To return to a balanced relationship there must be a period of
restoration.
Whoever causes the imbalance must be willing to submit to the
changes that
are required to take place.
Like a scale if balanced in a marital relationship is not restored the
one
sidedness will grow larger and larger and a true balance will never
be
achieved.
Hurt feelings, friction, and frustration will cause the wheels of
balance to be
stripped and a need for replacement will eventually occur.

STANDS TO REASON

In front of others never criticize your mate.
Doing so, you are determining your fate.
It is your criticalness that destroys your home.
In the end you will find yourself all alone.
Take the time to look at the problem in depth first.
This cooling off period could abstain you from hurt.
You can say, that in my house I make the calls.
Yet in front of your face the handwriting is on the wall.
To often we speak up in the name of freedom.
It is only words spoken out of love that stands to reason.

IN THE SHADOW

I was there I never came forward.
You may, at times see me but you never expressed it.
I looked to you for acknowledgement, yet I was overshadowed by
them.
Oh! How my heart ached to know if you glanced at me.
I looked as you rushed to and fro, never looking to see who is
watching, but
with confidence, you had it all, but did you?
did you not know you did not have it all, you didn't have me?
I didn't want you just yet, because I wanted you to give up all that
you held
dear, that I might come up out of the shadow.

TINTED

African-Americans come in many shades,
This was initiated during America's slave trade.

From the earliest of time my people had to struggle,
They were considered the no-named people in America's puzzle.

Their true color was not in their skin,
But their belief in God that lies deep within.

In early America's history, Black accomplishments weren't
mentioned.
Now, time and diversity are giving them hard-earned attention.

There have been roadblocks and laws to stop them at every turn.
Yet they kept moving forward, as others suffered and burned.

The foundation of my people is belief in the one true God.
Whose one and only Son was sacrificed and hung upon the cross.

We may not go down in history as owners of the house.
Because of these gifted people, America has global clout.

WORDS

Words can have a profound affect.
Words spoken can cause others to be blessed.
Words unspoken can be seen in a smile.
Words can encourage others to go an extra mile.
Words however spoken can determine your faith.
In giving one the word of life, it's never too late.
Words that you use must be carefully chosen.
Words can cause the callous heart to become unfrozen.
Words have power and can cut to the bone.
Words give you hope, courage, and healing to carry on.
The spoken word can be used for good or bad, life or death.
Which is what you'll get if you decided this will be your last
breath.

IT'S NOT OVER

We live to die.
If we have lived righteously, we shall be rewarded.
If we have lived the opposite…we shall also be rewarded.
The reward is given out in accordance with the way we lived.
The reward to the just will be out of this world.
The reward to the unjust will be the underworld.
You came into this world in the physical.
The final departure will be spiritual.
The coming and the going are beginnings with different endings.
You won't be the judge of the results.
You won't have the opportunity to be judgmental.
The Judge of all will make the decision minus your input.
Based on your merit, you no longer are covered by His grace.
He gave his all before you ever existed,
By not receiving His only One you will have missed it.

THE BARNYARD PIMP

Sitting in the yard and beneath a tree.
The old rooster had eyes centered on me.
The chickens were picking and scratching,
displaying their hen house ways.
The barnyard pimp was checking out all that was said.
He kept an eye on the young rooster of the yard,
always chasing him to ensure he knew he was boss.
Sometimes when the old rooster turned his back,
the minor pimp got into the act.
When the old rooster got into his game,
he stood on one leg and looked around
He'd run after a female chick and chased her down.
He would then walk and act like he's hip.
He'd kicked each foot out with proud strutting steps.
The old rooster made sure his brood didn't take him for a wimp.
When he walked you could tell he coveted the title of Barnyard
Pimp.

THE TELEPHONE

The telephone an extension of my ear.
A device that brings you joy as well as tears.
Some telephones have numbers in a circular type ring.
Others are touch-tone but accomplish the same thing.
We use the phone to keep in touch,
yet hearing the voice on the other end means so much.
The telephone has many tales to tell,
but as years passed the numbers have swelled.
It extends itself far and wide,
but into distance your voice can ride.
On lots of occasions when I am all-alone,
the telephone is the device that brings my love ones home.

SHE IS A BRICKHOUSE

Her firm foundation is dressed in curves.
It is her figure when she walks, she is heard.

You can see she is stacked from front to back.
She must be given respect as leader of the pack.

When she dances you are put in a trance.
As she moves her endowments, shows in her pants.

She is a brickhouse.

LET US THINK FOR OURSELVES

The sponsor started the contest talking trash.
His politics in the end was more viewers more cash.
The announcer started out saying this man would win.
His politics was to shape your mind before the event began.
I was determined to turn the television down low.
This would eliminate the sponsor and the announcers mind control.
The favorite had weak opponents handpicked.
This was part of the scheme of the matchmaker tricks.
In some bouts the best fighter didn't win.
This was determined before the event began.
Men of means need to act from the heart.
Instead, they figure anything can be bought.
Especially the public.

IN THE BAR

(Read as if you are rapping)

In the bar talking trash.
Yea, I got a plan
and I am fully sane
everything lines up
and I am ready to jam.

In the bar spending cash.
The green I got is good as gold
in my pocket I keep it fold
at the club I flash my stash

In the bar flashing my money
Ladies in the crowd seek to enjoy me.
I jumped around saying, "I am the man".
My wife comes up and pull my chain
saying, "If you want me, you must change your game".

In the bar telling jokes and being funny.
The lady of my life says, "I am your honey".
She never stops talking but says you've been warned
I am the woman you are taking home.
I looked at her, and she began to frown.
I dropped my head as if she put me down.

In the bar listening to the latest tune.
The spirit of joy removed the gloom.
Happiness filled me from head to toe,
as I danced and glided across the floor.
Looking for a special lady that make me crows.

IN THE BAR

In the bar talking trash.
In the bar spending cash.
In the bar flashing money.
In the bar pulling someone's honey.
In the bar listening to the latest tune.
In the bar dancing the jig, I reached for the moon.
In the bar doing my thing.
In the bar dancing the alligator and trying to sing.
In the bar looking left and looking right.
In the bar raising both hands seeking a fight.
In the bar talking smooth as butter
In the bar the ladies ran for cover.
In the bar drinking my drink.
In the bar so drunk I stink.
In the bar drinking from dawn to dusk.
In the bar off the stool I fell busting my butt.
Feeling real bad, I stumbled out the door.
Man, I was determined to drink no more.
Drunk and smelling like a skunk.

GRANDMOTHER

Grandmother, Grandmother, this is your day.
I thank God for you each night as I pray.
You were always there for me in my early years.
The comfort of your love removed my childhood fears.

God has blessed you with a life that is long.
Yet, you still give him the glory as he keeps you strong.
I haven't seen you in many years,
Looking forward to our reunion cause me to shed many tears.

You are oh! So special, that words cannot express.
You never gave up on me, as life put you to the test.
You are…special, like a fine wind, a loaf of bread, and a piece of
cheese all aged to
perfection.
You are like wine to be sipped and then swallowed; like bread to
be broken, yet shared;
like cheese preserved until ripen as one meditate on your presence.

You are special because there is no one else like you.
You may be imitated but not duplicated.
You are special because you are different, yet, like others, there is
sameness.
You are sturdy as a rock but your thought and concern for others
can be witnessed by
your tenderness.

In other words your humanness shines forth.
Your specialness is in the things you say and the deeds you have
done.
Life hasn't been easy, as you've stood the test of time.
Through your faith in God, you still have a sound mind.

Grandmother, this is your life.
Your perseverance has shown me how to be a good wife.

You have lived life on the physical, mental, and spiritual plan.
But it was God's wisdom you followed and not man.

Oh how the wind, the rain, and the hard times came but you
absorbed the shock.
You are the perfect role model as seen by your life.
For it is through your faith we've learned to fight the good fight.
May this day, forever be remembered, not because of the years you
have lived but the
truth and the specialness that radiates from you.

You have taught us to put our trust in God and obey his
commandments. Happy Birthday
Grandmother.

LADY OF THE HOUR

Mother Lawrence, one of a kind.
Mother Lawrence, one who speaks her mind.
A woman whose words are well thought.
A woman in conversation, who says, can we talk?
She answers the phone; Praise the Lord, Alice.
And God has blessed her in a home that looks like a palace.
The people and the business did their part.
Showing their love and giving from the heart.
She is quick to tell you she has Black, White, and Indian in her
genes.
Yet it is being in Gods love that makes her gleam.
Mother Lawrence a woman, who has experienced the loss of life,
She still has the spirit to fight the good fight
In all she does she gives honor to the Lord.
For she knows it is the love of the Lord, she is called.
It is the needy and others, she gives her mind, will, and emotions.
And it is the people who get filled by her love, caring, and true
devotion.

A lot of people talk but Mother Lawrence acts.
It is through this that I have established these facts.
Mother Lawrence knows what it is to endure pain.
Mother Lawrence, a woman who continues to stand by her man.
Her husband a true Christian warrior of the Lord, his name is Jake.
He is man of the house and she still fixes his plate.
She is quick to tell you it's not me but Gods power.
It's because of this she is the Lady of the Hour.

HE COME FROM AMONG US

Martin Luther King was a man heard and seen.
He believed life's problems were solvable dreams.
The nation had many dissenting factions.
He would rise and stir up righteous actions.
This man acted in an organized manner.
He was always up front carrying freedoms banner.
Martin should be considered America's savior.
He was about changing society's destructive behavior.
Though he did not have money as we call wealth.
His life was based around giving of himself.
This world makes claim and is full of chatter.
Martin showed love in his actions and nothing else mattered.
He centered his life around Jesus each night and each day.
His vision of true justice goes unfulfilled in this world's play.
He came from among us.

IN TRIBUTE TO MLK

PEOPLES CHOICE

Some people talk negative about Hilary and Bill.
These people kept the disadvantage in their will.
The GOP party was led by a man called Newt,
all his political decisions seemed to pollute.
He spoke Articulate with his mind.
In mediation he was the one that whined.
Hilary acted for health care from the heart.
Her adversaries acted in a way they can be bought.
Bill would always act on all's behalf.
The GOP action was based on who controls the cash.
As the GOP continues to make all the noise.
Bill and Hilary are still the people's choice.

THE FACE OF A CLOWN

He smiles.
He cries.
He also frowns.
He can hide behind a mask.
He is the face of a clown.
With his hands, he pantomimes.
He has different poses when he walks.
He makes various movements.
Yet he does not talk.
You can find him at the circus.
You can find him at the fair.
In all of his expressions,
you can feel that he cares.
The face of a clown.

WILLIE THE WEASEL

He would crack the window
Slowly, he'd peep through the blinds.
His ears like radar wanting to hear another's mind.
He'd turn the doorknob and pressed close to the wall.
His ears came to attention to hear it all.
We call him Willie, Willie the weasel.
Testimony he gives in court is considered legal.
Those who know him, he was sneaky and not loud
Everywhere people gathers he'd weasel into the crowd,
His mouth, always wide open, steadily jumped to the beat.
His gap tooth and laughter was really a treat.
Don't turn your back on him and always shoot from the hip.
You see, the weasel was always waiting for slip of your lip.
He loved to whisper gossip and his truth was all lies.
As he gathered information with large pop eyes.
The weasel was a weasel but he slithered around like a snake.
As he paid for information from those on the take.
Have you ever seen a prairie dog pop up and smell the air?
That's the weasel seeking a morsel of gossip and not want to share.
Most weasel like Willie will never stop.
Until you get mad and have to bust him out.

HE CAME GUNNING

(The Boxer)

The young gunfighter in the ring lacked skills.
The old gunfighter gave him a look that kills.

The old gunfighter circled right and circled left.
He chased the young warrior to see if he had depth.

The young gunfighter heard the applause of the crowd.
But the old gunfighter wanted to have the last bow.

The young fighter made it back to his corner.
His seconds told him more actions, or he'd be a goner.

During the next round the young warrior began to talk.
Yet the old gunner was beginning to stalk.

The young warrior threw a left and right hand fast.
When the smoke cleared, he was on his ass.

He struggled to his feet at the count of eight.
His legs had a wobble as he sought to escape.

The man who threw the punches is known as Pure Pain.
It was through his punching the young warrior forgot his name.

The old gunner was pumped up and showing clout.
It is still in his power to knock a man out.

The doctor was called into the ring.
Pure Pain was pumped up, doing his thing.

He wouldn't take a chance with the politics of boxing.
His mind was made up; he'd be the one doing the head knocking.

111

FEELINGS

My feelings give me extension of my existence.

I have the ability to go beyond myself and find that I am not alone.

My feelings create and nourish in me an emotional response.

The response may vary, hot or cold, pleasure or pain, but it gives my emotions life.

These feelings can create a sensitivity of tenderness found in love, fluctuate like an electrical impulse, to my mind, and is imprinted there.

Feelings are a part of you forever.

You can scrub your hands, you can wash your face, but you cannot remove the feeling.

You may want to forget the feeling but deep down in your existence the power to recall is there.

Things that happen below a visible threshold doesn't mean they don't exist.

We are becoming more just by the existence of living from day to day and forming meaning, by what we see, hear, taste, touch, and feel.

Only God knows the depth of my feelings.

NOTHING COMES EASY

Nothing comes easy, nothing. You struggle at first just to give meaning to living. When it doesn't come you are like the wind, blowin' to and fro, up and down. Your mind continuously searches your thoughts for meaning; otherwise you will find yourself catching another breeze blowing. When you have found meaning you must catch the fire of desire along the way. The desire must continuously be fed with success. Even with success desire can wane if you don't have a goal and love at the core of what you are striving.

Combining meaning, desire, and love to your endeavor will sustain you to cause you to enjoy the greatest pleasure. Whether it's your mental thoughts or the pushing of your physical body, you'll find yourself struggling to reach a desired end. In reaching your desired end you can have exhilaration in your heart, your thoughts and desire that can cause you to holler joyously and also cry. If the desire is not reached you can have a downswing, which also makes you cry. The cry of failure can also be seen outward or felt inwardly in the heart.

They may look the same to the on looker but to the recipient it is in the feeling that is felt throughout the individual being and imprinted on his heart according to the depth of his ability to feel.

CHICKEN

Is life really fair? Do you really know what the other fellow is thinking or where he is coming from? Is it all in the eyes of the beholder?

Well, once upon a time, in a far off exotic land, lived a large snake called Pete, The Python. He was 14 feet long and was housed in a big cage. When he killed it all happened by surprise attack to his prey. One particular day as Pete lay still in his cage, looking like a greenish brown tree that had been cut down; two plump chickens were introduced into his cage. As the chickens stepped on this unfamiliar tree (to them) their instincts caused them to be scared and flighty.

This was a strange environment to be in with a motionless python. Pete began to make slow sliding movement, which gave the appearance that he was taking the chickens for a ride as they walked upon the topside of this elongated form within the cage.

After one to two hours these feathered fowl began to become confident that there was no harm that would beset them. What a gross mistake! They didn't realize that Pete's earlier behavior was a disguise of deception because he was not hungry.

In a split second this humongous hulk became a mass of furious momentum as he curled and coiled around these fowls with fast violent powerful thrusting action. Thus, squeezing the breath of life right out of these chickens as their bones cracked in preparation for sucking down by unhinged jaws. What a sight for timid onlookers who cringed as Pete went on his eating binge.

This delicate twosome never knew what hit them for there was no advance warning. If they had lived to tell their story, it would probably be: "Trust your first instincts and be the chooser of your own fate and path, because you are no more." Afterwards, Pete went back to his unmoving, unassuming behavior.

Maybe Colonel Sanders was right in saying "Chicken is finger licking good: or in Pete's body language, "for snaking down the tube." Don't be fooled if you see no movement, for now this caged creature is chickenless.

MY TRIP HOME

My trip home was one of pain and one of anger, one of joy and one of peace. The Pain was to hear of the loss of most of my male classmates, who between the ages of 55 and 57, had departed the earthly world and those who were limited by poor health and strokes. The joy was seeing nieces and nephews who had matured into fine young women of substance and men who were now making their mark in their immediate community and the world bypassing the quick money bought about by corruption and drugs which has caused destruction to families, home, and death in some fashion all along the way. The peace was knowing they had accepted the Lord before they departed the world.

WHAT IS THERE TO LOOK FORWARD TO IN LIFE BESIDES GOD?

We live, we work, and we die. You live life from birth until death in this world. Some of us look for meaning in living. Others just flow along with the tides. In truth life seems at first a product of chance. In the beginning we are one of millions of sperms produced by the male struggling to penetrate the egg of the female. Everything there is has its own seed and egg clothed in its own glory. Yet nothing is made for nothing. All has its purpose. Each and everything shows Gods glory. To some of us, of the millions of sperms the strong survive and the weak fall by the wayside. The competition to survive is the first sign of your strength to live. The battle for life in a true sense is just the beginning and to us this should be a sign that faith and destiny guide us.

Not just our faith, but the faith of many others. The faith of Gods will for us, our mothers will to sustain us in the womb, and our individual faith to struggle to survive this inner environment. We are in God's sight, precious all along the way. Yet, He knew us before we ever were. He willed us as the forces of nature sought to destroy us. We competed to live and grow. As each of us grew in the womb, this gave us a time to fully develop and then be expelled to face the physical world and be a part of the natural things He's made.

As infants we are separated from but dependent on our mother to feed and care for us. Her loving care determines our growth and worth. As we go through life in certain stages and ages we think we are in control. Our personality begins to develop as time goes on. It seems like this personality has always been there. Love, growth, and development are taking place. Our ego, our pride, and selfishness give us a false sense that we are totally in charge. Look out! When you look back God's presence has always been with us and continues to guide us as well as those responsible for leading us.

So if we worship the Creator of all things, this shows God's power over the things that are made which includes man. He has instilled through His word what is right, what is wrong. Although we may veer away from Him, in the end, His will shall be done.

IN MY WORLD

In my world I don't have to say I love you verbally.
You would know love just by being in my presence.
Words would not have to describe it.
You would become alive by it.
The very heart of your soul would be uplifted.
Your face would shine like the sun.
I could reach out to you with my hand.
You would not have to meditate on what it meant.

You would know there is refuge in moving toward me as the void you had become full and your nakedness became cloth in the aura of my presence.

Removing all inhibition as you expressed your freedom to be yourself, knowing that you are accepted on the premise, I can be all that I am and not what others think I should be.

For my heart speaks and my soul accepts without doubt or fear lingering in my conscience as to what is right or wrong.

You would know without being touched, the defenselessness of my love for there never was a barrier, but a heart of acceptance.

You would be free to open the gates of your heart and pour out your thoughts, as I can not hide my selfish devotion, and you don't want to hold back in expressing your true emotions.

To speak to you of your love is good but to be attached to you emotionally is so much better.

There is a binding of our spirit and a oneness that only a look can determine our shared devotion for one another that causes us to find a solace forever.

THE MIND KNOWS

As I cradle her mind in the creases of my thoughts, I plowed into the seams of her senses and extracted the cleansing action of her love, as ripples of waves swelled in the charging current to her pulsating heart. She feasted hungrily in my well orchestrated touch, as I sifted the sweet nectar of tenderness from her emotions. I then triggered waves of wonderment that soothed her soul, as she sulked soothingly and patiently, as tears from the corners of each eye dropped with pleasure. Her cheeks began to slowly take on a glow that permeated her entire face with warmth and contented caring, as she languished in the dignity of her heartfelt desire of being smothered in the overpowering aroma given off by my stable assurance of love. She knew it was love as her mind totally accepted.

WHY NOT A SPANKING?

Who said children hate the rod? Think again, you children of the damned. It is a truth, spare the rod and spoil the child. God knows, I am glad there was a keeper of the house to restrict me in my youth so I could grow up with restraints, otherwise I would be the earth remains and to this day there would be no reason for rejoicing.

As a child I had ideas of sowing my oats or felt that I was physically tough and mentally strong to act as I pleased. Forgetting there was someone feeding me, clothing me, and schooling me. In living, children realize discipline through being talked to is just talk and they learn to ignore or become callus to what is said. But, when the old mans leather strap is just beyond the door, it will be a strong deterrent, fear sets in and behavior is controlled—at my house.

It had positive reinforcement on me to change for the better. A healthy fear of my elders is and should be necessary in the home and society. What gives me the right to do whatever I choose to do? Righteousness brings rewards and unrighteous behavior brings punishment. There is a price to pay for the deeds you do. It might come early in life. The acts will catch up with you. You pay in this world or the next.

It is the thoughts one holds about spanking that will determine if it is bad. As for me, it was good. For it informed me that I was restricted from doing certain actions that were negative to me now and the whole of society.

According to my father, who was a gentleman, his authority was shown through discipline, Gods authority bringing forth fear. This no less was the rule my father went by, that God gave him authority over his children. Fear of a parent is not restrictive, but creative. It instills respect, to give honor and the waiting for the right time in my life to act, which would be mainly for the betterment of society and myself.

POWER TO THE PEOPLE

You can't separate the elite in government from the elite in private enterprise. They come in many disguises. Yet the power of the people is controlled by a few. They may be millionaires, lawyers, philanthropists with political power who were voted into office on the strength of their money, political backing lobbyist or news media manipulation of our minds and our thoughts only to get for themselves at our expense. We are then controlled by laws, lawmakers, and law enforcers. These individuals take the soul of a nation and make decisions void of "In God We Trust". They ask for your labor and your vote and then hold you in a death lock that causes you to choke. Where is the politicians' heart? Whose soul has already been bought by the powers that be? Yes, you and I put him in power but he never could put them before him. He'll stand in your face and say we must do; yet his decision is based on one, himself. Politicians through their on ineptness unbalance the budget now we must balance it. We become part of the solution only when there is a political need, yet prior to, politicians didn't take heed.

Through the years jobs were eliminated by politicians and given to other countries without concern for the people who lost them. Yet we must not forget the power belongs to the people. We allow ourselves to be cast off while the politician who made the laws and broke the laws hid all their profits through write-offs.

The elitist will have you think that it is by them this country was built, but are they letting us also know that it is by them this country is being destroyed environmentally, economically, morally, and spiritually. Environmentally; destruction of the Rain Forest; economically; Jobs given to foreign shores, and morally and spiritually; God taken from the schools, government and churches of worship and allowing corruption to run rampant. They may be intellectually smart but their hearts are full of dead mens' bones (rotten) and with money they can be bought. Power must be returned to the people instead of abused by the few whose actions don't consider the whole hue. The government would have you think it is they who are rich and the people poor. It is just the opposite. Politicians refuse to see that the true solution to Americas problem to treat all people of America as one instead of putting race as a forerunner on all issues and decisions. Which in conclusion is not the best for the whole of our society or world. The people all of the world must wake up and tear corruption apart even if it requires making a new start. The meek must inherit the earth but with action that is forthcoming and used far and wide across this countries great divide. The power is the people. It must be taken and used righteously.

THE BRIDE AND GROOM

Relatives from the lightest shade to burnt Ivory all together under one roof giving honor to one of our future nieces who had come of age, celebrating at the Church of the Holy Comforter, holy matrimony in a lavish reception which could not even be overshadowed by the heat of the day. The brightness of the bride and groom twinkled with the stars as they danced together in the evening of the humid night. They sipped a drink from the same cup in a union where two separate individuals are now considered one. They can now enjoy life's highest privilege in which they can consummate the relationship where there is no doubt, no fear, and agreed to be right in the eyes of the only God now and forever. The bride sparkles with radiance as her gown which embraces her figure flows lovingly to her feet and like a peacock she strutted her stuff with style and elegance and driven to the heights of true love on earth that is second to none.

MY SISTER'S HOME

On the 2nd of July I slept at my oldest sister's home, Mary was determined to feed me. She is the mother figure of the family since my mother passed, always working hard and going to Church, she was determined to cook red beans and rice for me this day. I enjoyed this meal to the hilt. Later my other sister, Lydia arrived and we talked about the good times we've all had as sisters and brothers. Our hearts have always been filled with love for the family.

IN THE CLOUDS

As we hovered in brilliance of the clouds, their layers seemed to dance as if being chased by the wind. A layer of clouds below and a layer above drifted and shifted as we sped traveling toward our destiny. Other times you could see within the open spaces created as the clouds opened up and the mountain peaks pierced majestically through, exposing their vulnerability.

We continue to traverse the air as a continual blanket of clouds appearing as thick as sheep's wool remained still as if in a sleep. The sun at times would shine from above through the cloud causing them to take on the form of shimmering heat waves. What a magnificent view of the heavens and its splendid vastness.

Farther along we ran into clouds that were smooth looking and had humps shaped in a way that reminded you of a continuous ride on a sliding board as we then fell into unclouded air. Clouds, clouds, and more clouds, clouds of the purest white and looking as if herded together to unleash a downpour of water upon this part of the earth which they hung. Other times these clouds gave the appearance of being waves in the ocean rolling in a continuous path as if a mirage.

To comprehend man trying to put a limit on God when you look at the vastness of his creation is unfathomable. Harder still, to comprehend is why God would give to man, such a little creature, dominion over all things on the earth. Prior to landing, a rainbow, a rainbow appeared that seemed to be sitting on a cloud. My last thought! Wonderment.

BAYOU ST. JOHN

As I sat in my room in the cool of the evening, looking up on the water as it flowed with a ripple effect downstream in Bayou St. John. I could see the ducks hobbling up and down as they rode the forceful currents. At other times an alligator would make its presence known, mostly with only its eyes showing out of the water. Muskrats would travel close along the banks edge of the Bayou seeking what it could devour in its path. As the lightening flashed and the wind was furious, the activity among the creatures of the Bayou would pick up as if they were hurrying home or for a secured place from the predators of this environment.

TRIPPING AND HOPPING MY FLIGHT HOME

On the morning of October 5, 1998, I'd signed up at Elmendorf Air Force Base Passenger Terminal counter to begin my trip utilizing a military aircraft from Alaska Point Mogue Naval Air Station in California. Flying in military terminology is called "hopping". A flight is never a sure thing since it is based on a priority system and on a space available basis. You don't have to pay for the trip if you are a retired military man, but if you intend on having a box lunch, its cost is $3.00, which you may eat while flying.

To begin my trip I was awakened by my wife around 5:00 a.m. After packing my suitcase, I then placed it in the bed of my truck and departed my home for the flight aircraft terminal located on Elmendorf Air Force Base. The travel time from my home to Elemendorf Air Force Base was 20 minutes. The air this early morning was crisp and brisk about 35 degrees and the distance was 16 miles. This particular morning definitely was different, as I had drank an eight-ounce glass of apple cider vinegar, which had an affect on my bladder later in the day.

By arriving earlier than required at the terminal, I was informed that a C-17 aircraft was going to Travis Air Force Base, California with a check in time of 0830 a.m.; eight seats were available. I was also told, at 0715 a.m. this particular Sunday, that there was a C-130 aircraft with 54 seats available for personnel enroute to Point Mogue Naval Air Station; which is about 60 miles from Los Angeles International Airport. After a short waiting period I was manifested on this C-130 flight to Point Mogue. No box lunches could be manifested on this flight.

As time passed, the boarding call was announced over the P.A. system. Luggage was checked and x-rayed. I immediately reclaimed my carry-on luggage after personally being screened and was allowed to have a seat on the bus that was transporting all passengers to the awaiting aircraft. We arrived at the C-130 aircraft to find that all required maintenance checks had not been performed. The flight crew had not refueled the aircraft. Therefore, the Crew chief told the bus driver that 30 more minutes of ground time was needed. As time slowly passed, the pilot mentioned that all passengers were to return to the passenger terminal, as the aircraft seemed to have a problem originating in the fuel tank area. There was fuel leaking over a large area of the ground. The pilot did not know how long it would take to repair the leak and if it would cause a major delay or cancellation.

We were then ferried back to the terminal to wait on further instruction as to whether the flight would be canceled or it we would depart later. As you can see, a military flight is not a sure means of transportation, plus you never can be defrayed if you are looking for on-time departure and on-time arrival. On the other end of the spectrum, you don't have to pay for your trip; you can learn a great lesson in patience and get a cheap meal. After an hour had passed at the terminal the manifesting personnel made an announcement that the passengers on this scheduled flight should get ready to proceed to the outbound aircraft. We then checked out again, that is our carry-on luggage and personal items. We were then required to pass again through the scanner, whose alarm system went off because personnel had quite a few keys in their pockets or large belt buckles around their waists. As the first bus departed the terminal for our return trip to the runway, I began to feel the affect of the water, apple cider vinegar and honey, especially since I had taken a water pill for the reduction of fluid in my body earlier that morning.

On this second trip to the flight line to board the aircraft we had to travel around the perimeters of the Base to the other side of the runway which was stemming with wildlife. To my surprise, we experienced a mother moose along with her baby calf that was struggling to keep up. The mother at times stopped. It appeared she was giving her baby early morning exercise.

The driver of the bus radioed the passenger terminal personnel to be on the lookout for the presence of the moose approaching the runway in order to avoid an accident.

One thing I am sure of, I won't drink apple cider vinegar and honey in an eight-ounce glass of water on awakening in the morning. My reason for saying this is because after waiting in the cold yet seated on the bus for about twenty minutes before boarding the aircraft gave me such a strong desire to urinate. It gave me the feeling that my bladder would burst. During the time I sat on the bus I requested special permission from the pilot to board the aircraft to utilize the urinal since I couldn't wait any longer. I tried holding my breath, sitting up straight, all in the effort to relieve the ache- to no avail. I even crossed my legs and squeezed tight. The joke was on me, I felt like the parts of the body which said since I am the eye, I am more important than the feet. This was one time my bladder said it wanted relief because it knew it was not important and I agreed and sighed; oh, what a relief it is, knowing I either make it to the aircraft urinal or wet in my pants. There was no other choice to make.

Personnel on this flight consisted of active-duty personnel, wives of active duty personnel traveling with their children who had the Base Commanders permission to travel, that is, mothers whose husbands were on temporary duty in Saudi Arabia and other countries. There were also disabled veterans of military service, retired officers, and enlisted personnel, etc.

During the time the aircraft was airborne the pilot and crew personnel were very informative, we were allowed to look into the cockpit area as we were given the opportunity to stretch our legs. We were given earplugs to decrease the intensity of the noise in the C-130. As we reached our destination at Point Mogue Naval Air Station at 9:30 p.m. the flight personnel there were helpful in transporting all incoming personnel to billeting and downtown areas of Point Mogue.

I immediately saw the difference between a military hop and commercial airline. Military hops are free, commercial flights require money as well as paying tax fees. On this day my commercial flight was not much better than my hop except for the one having Turbine engines. While flying the crew gave each of us the opportunity to enter the cockpit area of the plane. The maintenance of gages was awesome and the navigator, pilot, and co-pilot went about performing their duties.

The flight was smooth from beginning to end. There was no turbulence. The landing an Point Mogue was great; there was a bus to meet us on arrival as we deplaned with our carry-on luggage. As we got on the bus we were the required to get off to retrieve it from the rear of the plane by a female senior NCO. We boarded the bus for a trip to the Base Opt Facility. The crewmembers were very helpful in helping the passengers to their respective destination by using their personal vehicles. After we reached our destination, one of the crewmembers was very instrumental in giving me a ride to the Billeting office. Rooms were $10.00 per night and well worth it. The rooms were great and looked with modern conveniences; bathrooms were beautiful with redwood furniture throughout. There were two televisions, one in the bedroom, and the other in the living room. There was a phone, VCR, personal coffeepot, and much, much, more; with a bed that allowed you to sleep like a baby, cuddled in the warmth of a mother's arms, or a husband in the arms of his wife. The Base was beautiful. The Navy owns the tenant portion but part of it is used for flying purposes and is rented to the Air Force. I thank God for such a safe flight and timely arrival. Right across from my room was a McDonalds restaurant on the Base of Point Mogue.

After waiting an hour for a taxi at Base Billeting at Point Mogue, I called the Yellow Cab taxi again, since he had not arrived earlier. He informed me he had gone to another destination by the same name. The driver then came to the Billeting Office and loaded my luggage, at which time I entered the taxi for a trip to Cammerillo to catch a bus to Los Angeles Airport. Along the road to Cammerillo were large areas of vegetation growing. This part of California was agriculture at its best, in a state of sunshine and rain, concrete and dirt roads. While in Cammerillo , I had a cup of coffee and a piece of cheesecake; here I met a friendly waitress named Cheryl. Out of the kindness of her heart she walked down to the bus stoop to get me a copy of the bus schedule, only to find there were none left. As I continued to eat my cheesecake and drink a cup of coffee. I gave her a copy of a book of poems I had written, "Through Ebony Eyes" and "You Got Me Going In Circles", for which she was very thankful. I then walked back to the bus stop for my 11:20 p.m. bus ride to LAX terminal.

As the bus traveled the freeway from Cammerillo to Thousand Oaks, the highways caused they bus to loose speed because of the higher altitude. The bus was limited to a locked in speed of 70 miles an hour. Once we hit level road, the speed increased dramatically. California has some the most pristine highways to travel. As we went down Thousand Oaks Boulevard, the sun beamed down, but we were lucky to be inside an air-conditioned bus. We then returned to Highway 101 to Los Angeles Airport. Enroute there were dips and valleys all along the road. There were trees pressed together, like tapered Christmas trees reaching for the sky. Five lane highways going one way were filled with traffic. As we reached Woodland the bus drive collected the $19.00 fee for the trip. Once we reached our destination at the airport my first stop was at Southwest Airlines, this was my stop. I then got in a line that was quite long to purchase a commercial airline ticket. Luck was on my side because I did not have reservations and there was such a large crowd. The flight got a bit bumpier from Los Angeles as we approached the Phoenix Airport this was due to the large amount of hot air that was present. Once arriving in Houston we had a 15-minute wait before departing for New Orleans. This area of the flight to New Orleans went smooth including loading the plane. We picked up one passenger as we were on our way to the city of the Mardi Gras and partying. It was dark when we arrived at the place where you can be loosing a football game and afterwards win in having a treat at a party celebrating the loss.

IN THE END

Jesus Christ, the Son in whom payment is due, stated we must worship the Father in spirit and truth. Our bodies are the temples in which he dwells. His word, in our hearts is what delivers us from hell. The soul of man consists of his mind, will and emotions when renewed will allow us to give faithful devotion. The body in the end goes back to dust. It is from the dust we begin and were brought forth. Our spirit, the inner man will rise to be with God. This is our reward promised by Jesus of his everlasting love.

ABOUT THE AUTHOR

Ivery L. Henderson was born in New Orleans, Louisiana, on December 7, 1941. He was the second son of Mary and Louis Henderson. He attended McDonogh #27 and Jefferson Parish for his grade school years. He attended high school at L.B. Landry in the greater New Orleans area. He was co-captain of their football team. He was a member of two State Champion football teams. He was captain of the track team during his senior year and was the Student Council president.

After graduating he enlisted in the US AIR FORCE and attained the rank of Master Sergeant and was stationed in Europe, Asia, Alaska, and much of the lower 48, including Michigan, California, and Louisiana. His first love became boxing and he excelled, becoming a lightweight and a light welterweight champ. He also accumulated over 120 college credits during this period of his life.

This book is written from a black man's perspective, based on his life experiences and his attempts to be objective in that area. He tell that although newspapers may write about daily happenings, in his feelings, and in his heart and his soul he is greatly affected by the rhythm of the happenings taking place around and to him. His interpretation of life is that it is an integral part of society that causes him to reach out and witness the spirit of rejection. Yet, he sees that God proves to be his greatest strength and weapon to overcome the physical and spiritual realm, in a world where money can corrupt the souls of man.

His poems may give you a view of truth, justice, and righteousness prevailing in a society where racism and political corruption is witness to the actions of men. Where worth is determined by money. It should show the reader how to look at life events that came make you, shape you, or break you. That the choice to love or hate lies with the individual whether the problem is caused by an individual or society in general.

If the Spirit of the Lord is leading you, you will overcome.

www.ingramcontent.com/pod-product-compliance
Lightning Source LLC
Chambersburg PA
CBHW051411280526
45785CB00003B/1026